Amazing Homes
We Choose To Live In

商務印書館（香港）有限公司
http://www.commercialpress.com.hk

CENGAGE
Learning™

Australia • Brazil • Japan • Korea • Mexico • Singapore • Spain • United Kingdom • United States

Amazing Homes We Choose To Live In 非常家園

Director of Content Development:
Anita Raducanu
Series Editor: Rob Waring
Editorial Manager: Bryan Fletcher

Associate Development Editors:
Victoria Forrester, Catherine McCue
責任編輯：冼懿穎

出版：

商務印書館（香港）有限公司
香港筲箕灣耀興道3號東匯廣場8樓

Cengage Learning
Units 808-810, 8th floor,
Tins Enterprises Centre,
777 Lai Chi Kok Road, Cheung Sha Wan,
Kowloon, Hong Kong

網址：http://www.commercialpress.com.hk

http://www.cengageasia.com

發行：香港聯合書刊物流有限公司
　　　香港新界大埔汀麗路36號中華商務
　　　印刷大廈3字樓

印刷：勝利印務私人有限公司
版次：2009年7月第1版第1次印刷

ISBN: 978-962-07-1865-6

出版說明

本館一向倡導優質閱讀，近年連續推出以 "Q" 為標誌的優質英語學習系列(*Quality English Learning*)，其中《Black Cat 優質英語階梯閱讀》，讀者反應令人鼓舞，先後共推出超過60本。

為進一步推動閱讀，本館引入Cengage 出版之*Footprint Library*，使用*National Geographic*的圖像及語料，編成百科英語階梯閱讀系列，有別於Black Cat 古典文學閱讀，透過現代真實題材，百科英語語境能幫助讀者認識今日的世界各事各物，擴闊視野，提高認識及表達英語的能力。

本系列屬non-fiction (非虛構故事類)讀本，結合閱讀、視像和聽力三種學習功能，是一套三合一多媒介讀本，每本書的英文文章以headwords寫成，headwords 選收自以下數據庫的語料：*Collins Cobuild The Bank of English*、*British National Corpus* 及 *BYU Corpus of American English* 等，並配上精彩照片，另加一張video/audio 兩用DVD。編排由淺入深，按級提升，只要讀者堅持學習，必能有效提高英語溝通能力。

商務印書館(香港)有限公司

編輯部

使用説明

百科英語階梯閱讀分四級，共八本書，是彩色有影有聲書，每本有英語文章供閱讀，根據數據庫如 *Collins Cobuild The Bank of English*、*British National Corpus* 及 *BYU Corpus of American English* 選收常用字詞編寫，配彩色照片及一張video/audio 兩用DVD，結合閱讀、聆聽、視像三種學習方式。

讀者可使用本書：

 學習新詞彙，並透過延伸閱讀(Expansion Reading)
練習速讀技巧

 聆聽錄音提高聽力，模仿標準英語讀音

 看短片做練習，以提升綜合理解能力

Grammar Focus解釋語法重點，後附練習題，供讀者即時複習所學，書內其他練習題，有助讀者掌握學習技巧如 scanning, prediction, summarising, identifying the main idea

中英對照生詞表設於書後，既不影響讀者閱讀正文，又具備參考作用

Contents 目錄

The CD-ROM contains a video and full recording of the text

CD-ROM 包括短片和錄音

Words to Know

This story is set in Italy on the island of Sicily. It happens near the city of Catania, around a volcano called Mount Etna.

(A) A Volcano. Read the paragraph. Then label the picture with the correct form of the <u>underlined</u> words.

A volcano is a mountain with a large hole at the top which is called a <u>crater</u>. A large volcano may have hundreds of smaller craters, or <u>cones</u>, on its sides. In an <u>eruption</u>, volcanoes produce very hot, melted rock. When it is under the ground, this hot, melted rock is called <u>magma</u>. Once it comes out of the volcano, the hot rock is called <u>lava</u>. Lava, smoke, and gas come out of a volcano during an eruption. This makes the area around a volcano a dangerous place!

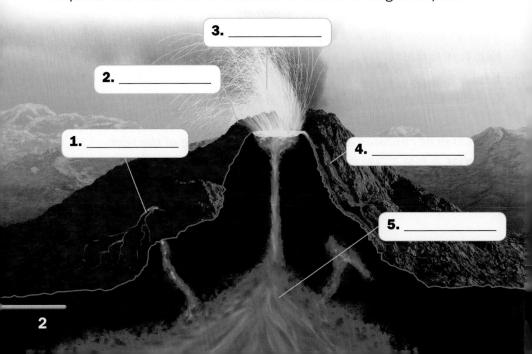

3. _____

2. _____

1. _____

4. _____

5. _____

B Studying Volcanoes. Read the definitions. Then complete the paragraph with the correct form of the words.

> **crust:** another term for the earth's surface
> **unpredictable:** often changing; impossible to guess
> **volcanic ash:** very fine rock that comes out of a volcano during an eruption
> **volcanologist:** a scientist who studies volcanoes
> **tectonic plate:** one of the many large, moving pieces under the earth's surface

Scientists known as (1)_____ study a number of different features of volcanoes. They study the movement of (2)_____ deep under the earth. They also study how these movements formed volcanic openings in the earth's (3)_____ long ago. When a volcano erupts, these scientists examine the lava and (4)_____ that come out of it. They want to know why volcanoes erupt so that they can protect people who live near them. It's difficult to know what these (5)_____ creations will do next!

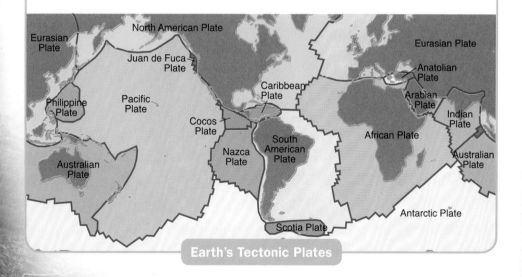

Earth's Tectonic Plates

When Sicily's Mount Etna **erupts**[1], it really is a beautiful sight. It looks like an amazing, powerful fireworks display and it's the kind of show that everyone notices. However, there's one audience that's watching the volcano for a different reason.

It's a small group of scientists who have made watching Mount Etna their life's work. They're volcanologists, and their job is to be on Mount Etna and to watch it very closely.

---

[1]**erupts:** throws out a lot of hot rocks and ashes

Skim for Gist

Read through the entire story quickly to answer the questions.

1. What is the story basically about?

2. Why is Salvatore Caffo important to the story?

Salvatore Caffo is the main volcanologist on Mount Etna. From his office at Mount Etna National Park, Caffo has an excellent view of the power of the volcano. It's the best place for him to do his job. Caffo's responsibility is to watch the unpredictable mountain and keep records of its activity.

Mount Etna, or simply 'Etna', is more than 10,000 feet high, which makes it Europe's highest active volcano. The loud noises, smoke, and gas that come from the mountain remind everyone that Etna is active. It could erupt at any time.

Caffo grew up in the city of Catania, which is less than 30 miles down the mountain from Etna's craters. He was always extremely interested in the mountain, even as a young boy. He says that when he was just 11 years old, he knew that he wanted to make volcanoes an important part of his life.

At Mount Etna National Park, Caffo's task is important. He must work towards understanding the volcano's role on the planet Earth. He must also help others to understand it. Why is this so important? Because, on Etna, there's a very close relationship between man and volcano. There are many people who live on and around this active volcano, so it's very important to always know what's happening.

In Caffo's words: 'Mount Etna is a mountain where there's a very strong **interaction**[1] between man and nature. You can't **leave that out of the equation**[2].'

---

[1] **interaction:** two or more things coming together and affecting each other
[2] **leave (sth) out of the equation:** fail to consider an issue when making a decision or planning

Infer Meaning

1. Who is Caffo referring to when he uses the word 'man'?

2. According to Caffo, what fact about Etna must be remembered?

9

Man and nature have lived together on Mount Etna for centuries, but the volcano has been around for far longer. Mount Etna began to form 600,000 years ago. It began at the place where the African and Eurasian tectonic plates come together, deep under the surface of the earth. On Etna, there are more than 100 craters and cones in a huge volcanic area. These craters and cones indicate the places where gases and magma escape from under the earth's crust.

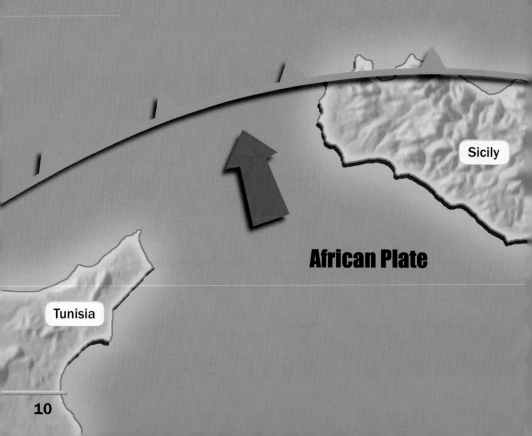

Sicily

African Plate

Tunisia

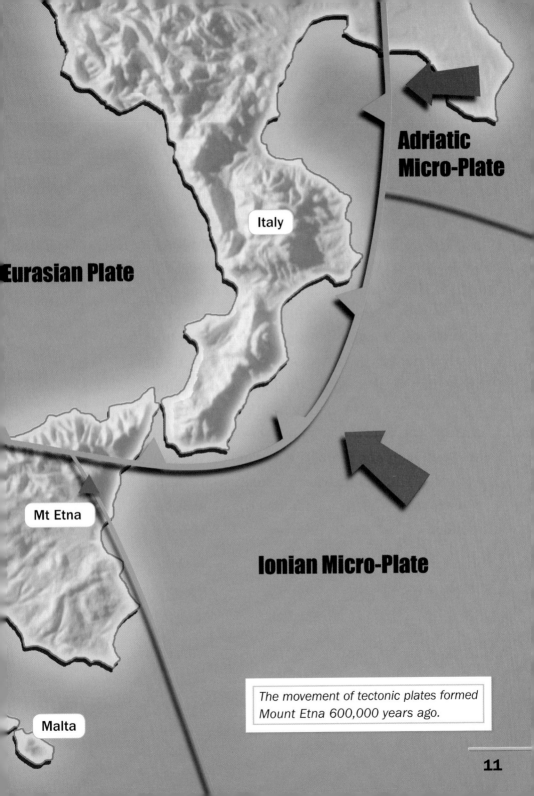

Adriatic
Micro-Plate

Italy

Eurasian Plate

Mt Etna

Ionian Micro-Plate

Malta

The movement of tectonic plates formed
Mount Etna 600,000 years ago.

Today, thousands of people live on and around the volcano. The volcanic ash makes excellent farmland. For centuries, people have been farming the rich volcanic earth and growing their food near the volcano. Now, many people are also making money from tourists who come to see the eruptions.

Although people have been living on Etna for a long time, it doesn't mean that it's an easy place to live. The town of Nicolosi is just 12 miles down the hill from the crater. The village was first built more than 800 years ago, but eruptions from Etna have destroyed it twice. The people who live in the village know that Nicolosi could be destroyed by Etna again. Yet, the town also benefits from being so close to the volcano. It's an interesting relationship between man and land. The **mayor**[1] of Nicolosi explains: 'There is the risk. We know that. We are **conscious of**[2] this risk. If it's destroyed, well, we rebuild.'

[1]**mayor:** leader of a town or city
[2]**(be) conscious of:** know about

Nicolosi is not the only town in the area that the volcano has affected. There are over 20 small towns which lie around the bottom of the volcano. Zafferana Etnea is one of them. It is eight miles from Nicolosi and on the southeastern side of Mount Etna. It's another town that knows the dangers of the volcano very well.

In 1991, an eruption started on Etna which lasted more than 400 days. It covered a whole valley that is near Zafferana Etnea with lava. The woods, fields, animals, and water were all covered by a red-hot flow of lava. When the people of Zafferana Etnea saw the lava, they were terrified that it was going to reach their town and destroy it.

In 1991, a 400-day eruption of Etna nearly covered an entire valley.

In the end, the lava flow stopped just a few hundred metres from the town. Now, there is a **religious statue**[1] at the place where the lava stopped. People go there to give thanks that the town was saved.

Living so close to Mount Etna has caused people in the area to accept the danger. They know that the volcano will erupt again. It can't be avoided. They just don't know when it will happen — maybe today, maybe tomorrow. One man who lives in Zafferana Etnea feels that in 1991, it was their turn to be in danger. But, he adds, the next time it may be another town. 'That time it was us. This time it's them,' he says. 'Maybe in ten years it will be Linguaglossa's turn, or Randazzo's — it's like that. You get used to it. You live with it, and so it doesn't **scare**[2] you.'

---

[1] **religious statue:** a figure which represents a culture's beliefs in a god or gods
[2] **scare:** make sb afraid

The people who live around Etna understand the volcano because they are so close to it. They realise that the volcano plays an important role in life on Earth. In fact, according to Caffo, volcanoes are an important part of the world's environmental system. If there were no Etna, life on Earth would be very different. 'I hope that people understand the big importance of this **thermodynamic**[1] machine,' he says. 'Without [the] volcano, there isn't … life.'

---

[1]**thermodynamic:** connected to the relationship between heat and other types of energy

For some, the volcano plays another important role; this time it's a social one. It can help people to understand their own place, or their role in life on Earth. Caffo spends much of his time walking around the volcano. He often explores the black land that is covered with dried lava and examines the ancient craters. For him, Etna influences his approach to life in general. It reminds him of the fact that he is very small when he compares himself with the size of the earth!

Mount Etna is always changing, so it is very interesting for volcanologists. The Piano del Lago cone, for example, is Etna's newest feature. It erupted for the first time in July, 2001. When it erupted, it was truly amazing. The pressure was so powerful that lava shot a quarter of a mile into the air! Huge black clouds of smoke and ash erupted out of the crater, as gases from deep within the earth were released.

100 metres

In 2001, Mount Etna erupted and lava shot about a quarter of a mile into the air!

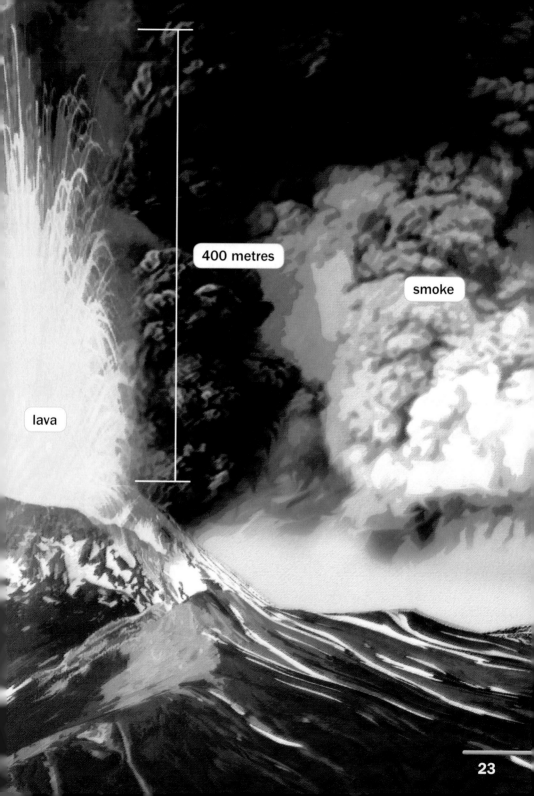

400 metres

smoke

lava

On Etna, there is always something new for Caffo to study. He works with mountain guides and other scientists to survey Etna's eruptions. He tests the lava, measures gases, and looks for surface changes. These elements can provide signs of what is happening under the earth.

Etna has technically been active since 1995, and any eruption is still very exciting for volcanologists. 'When you smell the **sulphur**[1] in the air, it gives you **shivers down your spine**[2]! This is the birth, the creation of new earth,' explains Caffo.

---

[1]**sulphur:** a yellow chemical element that smells bad
[2]**shivers down (one's) spine:** shakes because you are cold or afraid

Sequence the Events

What is the correct order of the events?
Write numbers.

_____ The town of Nicolosi was built.

_____ The Pian del Lago cone erupted.

_____ Mount Etna first formed.

_____ There was an eruption that lasted more than 400 days.

Caffo explains that it's not easy to know what the volcano will do next. Even with all of their studies, scientists still don't always understand what's happening deep within the earth. Mount Etna remains as unpredictable as it has always been. For Caffo and the other scientists who study it, that's part of their interest. If they always knew Etna's next move, their job wouldn't be very challenging. In the end, it's Mount Etna's surprises that make Caffo's job exciting. Nobody knows what Etna will do next!

After You Read

1. When does the small group of scientists watch Mount Etna?
   A. in the morning
   B. annually
   C. twice a week
   D. all the time

2. Smoke from Mount Etna shows that it is an active volcano
   A. True
   B. False

3. What view is expressed by Salvatore Caffo on page 8?
   A. People should not live near Etna.
   B. Man and nature are linked.
   C. People forget about the volcano.
   D. Nature is stronger than man.

4. Match the cause to the effect.
   Effect: A volcano is formed.
   A. Magma flows down.
   B. A crater erupts.
   C. Tectonic plates come together.
   D. Gases come out from the earth.

5. For the people in Nicolosi, living near Etna has both _____
   and _____.
   A. benefits, risk
   B. farmlands, mountains
   C. benefits, good points
   D. mountains, hills

6. How many small towns are there near Mount Etna?
   A. two
   B. eight
   C. twenty
   D. four hundred

7. Which of the following is a good heading for page 16?
   A. Which Town Is Next?
   B. Randazzo Saved
   C. Eruption Happens Again
   D. People Are Scared

8. On page 19, Caffo calls Etna a 'machine' because the volcano:
   A. is not natural
   B. has a job
   C. destroys the environment
   D. is near people

9. What's the main point on page 20?
   A. to describe the volcano in detail
   B. to present Caffo's emotions
   C. to talk about people's size
   D. to show the volcano's effect on people

10. What happened when the Piano del Lago cone erupted?
   A. Ash shot a mile into the air.
   B. Etna's oldest feature was made.
   C. Lava exploded from the crater.
   D. Red smoke went high in the sky.

11. In the second paragraph on page 24, 'this' refers to:
   A. an eruption
   B. sulphur
   C. an active volcano
   D. a scientist

12. Scientists consider Etna's action to be:
   A. logical
   B. challenging
   C. simple
   D. predictable

Volcanoes
ON THE MOON

Researchers are very knowledgeable about the nature of the Moon. They have taken detailed photographs and space travellers have brought rocks back from the Moon's surface. By studying these, scientists have discovered that the Moon has had many volcanic eruptions in the past. They have also found that volcanoes on the Moon are very different from those on Earth.

The Moon and Earth both have volcanoes.

Age and Position of Volcanoes on Earth and the Moon

Although both sites have experienced significant volcanic activity, there are clear differences between them. There are still many active volcanoes on Earth that could erupt at any time. Most of the volcanoes on Earth are about 100,000 years old. However, the Moon's volcanoes are between three and four billion years old and are no longer active. A second major difference is their position. Volcanoes on Earth are fairly evenly distributed around the tectonic plates. Most of the Moon's volcanoes are on only one side.

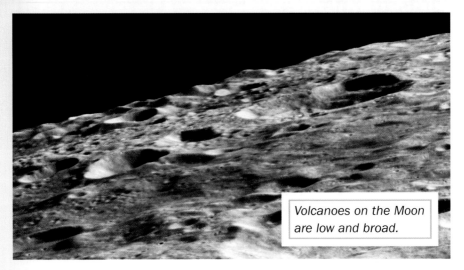

Volcanoes on the Moon are low and broad.

The Influence of Tectonic Plate Activity

Volcanologists look carefully at tectonic plate activity. On Earth, volcanic activity usually happens very close to mountains. This is where the movement of tectonic plates is the strongest. On the Moon, however, there doesn't seem to be any tectonic plate activity. Instead, the volcanoes seem to occur wherever the crust of the Moon is thinnest. Scientists have suggested that the crust is thinnest on the side of the Moon that is closest to Earth. This could be one reason why many volcanoes are found there.

Size and Shape of Volcanoes on Earth and the Moon

On Earth, there are many tall volcanoes. Tall volcanoes are formed by strong eruptions with many layers of volcanic ash and lava. This results in a cone-shaped volcano with an empty crater inside. On the Moon, however, the eruptions were gentler. Therefore, the results were quite different — a broad, thin coating of lava over the surface of the Moon. This created the low, wide volcanoes which we find there.

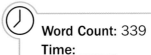

Word Count: 339
Time: _____

Words to Know

This story is set in South America. It starts near Brazil and goes through the country of Venezuela. It happens on the Orinoco River.

VENEZUELA

ATLANTIC OCEAN

Orinoco R.

NORTH AMERICA

SOUTH AMERICA

BRAZIL

N
W—E
S

 A **Landscapes of the Orinoco.** Read the definitions and look at the picture below. Write the number of the correct <u>underlined</u> word next to each item.

1. The <u>sea</u> is a very large body of water.
2. A <u>delta</u> is the place where a big river enters the sea.
3. <u>Mountains</u> are very high areas of land.
4. A <u>plain</u> is a large area of flat land.
5. A <u>waterfall</u> is a place where water falls from a higher area.
6. A <u>river</u> is a large body of water that moves in one direction.
7. A <u>stream</u> is a small body of water that moves in one direction.
8. A <u>rainforest</u> is a large area of trees and other plants where it rains a lot.

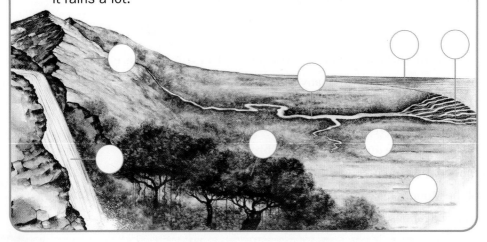

B **Animals of the Orinoco.** Here are some wild animals you will find in the story. Label the picture with the words in the box.

anaconda
capybara
crocodile
jaguar
piranha

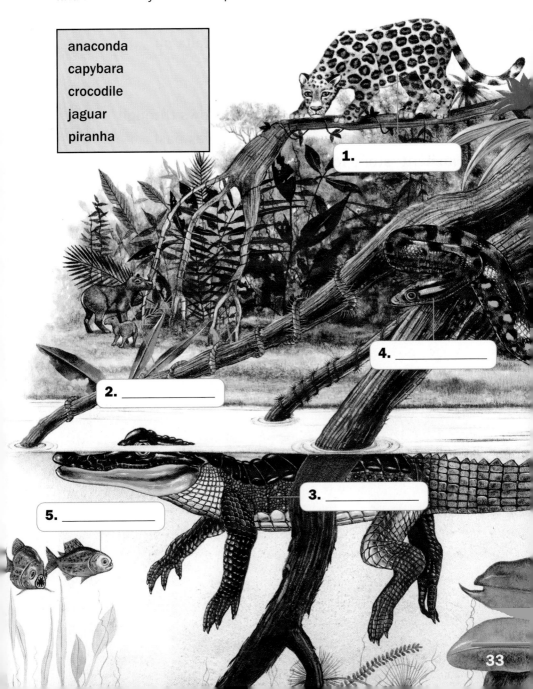

1. _____

2. _____

3. _____

4. _____

5. _____

The Orinoco River in South America is one of the longest rivers in the world. It starts in the mountains of Venezuela and Brazil. It then flows for nearly 1,300 miles to its delta on the Atlantic Ocean.

Part 1

On its way south, the Orinoco flows through many different **landscapes**[1]. It moves past **ancient**[2] stone formations, over waterfalls, through rainforest areas, and across large plains.

---

[1]**landscapes:** what you can see when you look across an area of land
[2]**ancient:** very old

The Orinoco Delta is the area where the river's water flows into the sea. The area around the delta is full of streams and small rivers. These smaller rivers, or **tributaries**[1], connect to the larger Orinoco. One of these tributaries, called the Caroni, features Angel Falls. Angel Falls is the highest waterfall in the world!

---

[1]**tributary:** a small river that flows into a larger river

Angel Falls, which is on the Caroni tributary, is the highest waterfall in the world.

However, there's more than just water in the delta. The Orinoco Delta is also home to several South American Indian cultures. They have lived next to the river for thousands of years and they still live there today. Actually, the name 'Orinoco' comes from a local language. It means 'place to **paddle**'.[1]

One of these Orinoco Indian cultures is the Yanomami. About two thousand Yanomami people live near the river, far from the rest of the world. For them, and about twenty other local cultures, the Orinoco is an important **natural resource**.[2] The river not only gives them a means of travel, but also a supply of clean water and food. The Orinoco River greatly supports these traditional cultures.

---

[1] **paddle:** move a small boat through water with a short piece of flat wood
[2] **natural resource:** sth which naturally exists in a place and can be used by people

a waterway

a paddle

The rainforest around the Orinoco River has many kinds of plants and animals. It is home to more than a thousand different types of birds. In the river itself, there are many types of fish — including the dangerous **piranha**[1]! And on the land around the river, you'll find even more interesting animals...

---

[1] **piranha:** a kind of fish with sharp teeth and a desire to eat meat

… like the Orinoco crocodile. He may have a big smile, but be careful! These animals can grow to more than 18 feet long! This makes the Orinoco crocodile one of the longest crocodiles in the world.

There are big snakes on the Orinoco River too. One of the biggest is the **anaconda**[1]. It's one of the largest kinds of snakes in the world.

In the rainforest, you may have a chance to see one of the area's beautiful **jaguars**[2]. But on the open plains, you will more likely see a totally different animal — the world's biggest **rodent**[3], the capybara.

---

[1] **anaconda:** a large, non-poisonous snake
[2] **jaguar:** a large, wild cat with yellow fur and black spots
[3] **rodent:** a kind of small animal with long, sharp teeth

Scan for Information

Scan page 42 to find the correct information.

Where do these animals live — in the rainforest, around the river, or on the plains?

1. crocodiles _____

2. anacondas _____

3. jaguars _____

4. capybaras _____

Part 2   Over the past fifty years, things have changed along the Orinoco River. Some of the cities and towns have grown significantly. These cities have also taken some of the land where animals and plants once were. The new industrial world is slowly coming to the Orinoco Delta. But what industries have been introduced? More importantly, what are they doing to the beautiful river, its animals, and its people?

Identify the Main Idea

1. What is the main idea of the paragraph on page 45?

2. What are two pieces of information that support this idea?

One of the industries that has grown is electricity production. Parts of the Orinoco now have **dams**[1] to help control the water. These dams also collect the river's water to create electrical power.

There are also other industries in the area as well. Companies there have found valuable products, like gold, diamonds, and oil. Very big ships now travel up and down the river from the Atlantic Ocean to move these products from place to place.

---

[1]**dam:** a strong wall built across a river to stop the water

a dam

gold

diamonds

oil

a ship

It's clear that there have been some big changes on the Orinoco in recent years. But not everything has changed. Many sections of the river and the areas around them have stayed almost the same. The people of Venezuela want to continue to enjoy the river's beauty and animals.

There are now several national parks and rainforest **reserves**[1] in the delta. These parks and reserves will help this great river remain an important natural resource for Venezuela. For now, the great Orinoco River is safe. It can continue to support the birds, animals, and people that depend on it.

---

[1]**reserve:** an area of land used to protect wild plants and animals

After You Read

1. The Orinoco River flows _____ the mountains _____ the sea.
   A. under, into
   B. down, from
   C. from, to
   D. to, and

2. A good heading for page 38 is:
   A. River Only Offers Means of Travel
   B. People Lived by River for Hundreds of Years
   C. Orinoco Only Helps Yanomami Culture
   D. River Is Important to Local Cultures

3. The writer thinks the rainforest is sometimes _____ and always _____.
   A. varied, safe
   B. dangerous, interesting
   C. quiet, dry
   D. quiet, safe

4. Why is the jaguar special?
   A. It is the biggest rodent in the world.
   B. It is the longest animal in the world.
   C. It is a large type of snake.
   D. none of the above

5. On page 42, 'it's' refers to a
   A. crocodile
   B. capybara
   C. anaconda
   D. jaguar

6. The cities and towns along the delta show that the area is:
   A. totally natural
   B. changing
   C. very quiet
   D. staying the same

7. On page 45, the phrase 'have grown significantly' can be replaced by:
   A. have grown a lot
   B. have not really grown
   C. have reduced in size
   D. have stayed the same size

8. What is one of the benefits of the dams?
   A. Electrical power is produced.
   B. The water cannot be controlled.
   C. Oil companies are making money.
   D. Ships are coming from small towns.

9. Oil and diamond companies are both signs of industry coming to the delta.
   A. True
   B. False

10. According to page 48, what is the purpose of the rainforest reserves in the delta?
   A. So people can create more industry.
   B. To protect the natural area.
   C. To support local people.
   D. To help the towns and cities.

11. The Orinoco River must continue to support the _____ and _____ living near it.
   A. oil, diamonds
   B. ships, companies
   C. towns, cities
   D. animals, people

'Exploring Our World'

an interview with Dr. Bernard Thompson

Judy: Hello. This is Judy Jamison here with our weekly science programme, 'Exploring Our World.' Here to talk with us this week is the well-known scientist, Dr. Bernard Thompson. In 2006, Dr. Thompson spent a year in the Amazon Rainforest studying the local plant and animal life. Welcome, Dr. Thompson!

Dr. Thompson: Thank you, Judy. I'm happy to be here.

Judy: So, can you tell us a little about your work?

Dr. Thompson: Certainly! I'm interested in helping protect all forms of life in the forest. This includes everything from the beautiful jaguars on the land, to the piranhas in the rivers. We also want to protect their environment as well. We want to save the trees that make up the rainforest and keep the rivers clean.

Judy: And what did you learn on your latest trip?

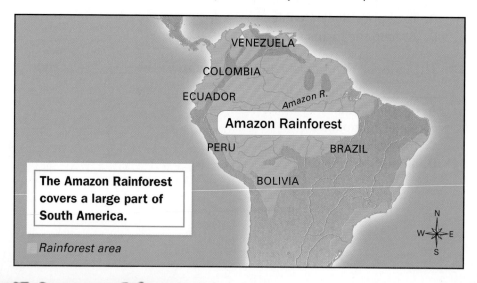

VENEZUELA

COLOMBIA

ECUADOR

Amazon R.

Amazon Rainforest

PERU

BRAZIL

BOLIVIA

The Amazon Rainforest covers a large part of South America.

Rainforest area

N
W — E
S

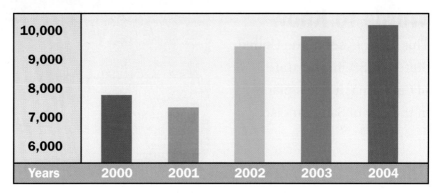

Square Miles of Rainforest Lost Each Year

Dr. Thompson:	Unfortunately, I learned some things that really worried me. Did you know the rainforest is becoming smaller and smaller every year? Data shows that in the year 2000, the area lost about 7,500 square miles of forest. In 2004, we lost over 10,000 square miles!
Judy:	What are the causes of this?
Dr. Thompson:	Some large companies are cutting down a lot of the trees. They want to get to the natural resources in the area. Some are looking for oil. Others are looking for gold and diamonds. Farmers are also clearing a lot of the land. Wood from the trees has also become a valuable product all over the world. It's a big problem!
Judy:	Yes, it sounds serious.
Dr. Thompson:	It is. And in order to help people get these valuable resources, some governments are building roads. These roads are bringing more people and machines to the area. This means that the rainforest will continue to be cut down quickly.
Judy:	What will happen if the current situation doesn't change?
Dr. Thompson:	Well, according to recent theories, the rainforest could be gone within 30 years...

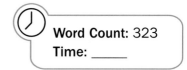

Word Count: 323
Time: _____

Words to Know

This story is set in the United States (U.S.), in the state of California. It takes place in the city of San Francisco.

 A Multicultural Neighbourhood. Read the paragraph. Then complete the sentences with the correct form of the <u>underlined</u> words.

This story is about an old <u>neighbourhood</u> in San Francisco called the Mission District or The Mission for short. This neighbourhood started near a <u>church</u> called Mission Dolores. Spanish <u>missionaries</u> started the church in 1791. They wanted to teach people about their beliefs. Now, many people from other countries live in The Mission. The majority of these <u>immigrants</u> are <u>Latino</u>. They come from Central and South America. This has made the <u>community</u> that lives in the area very <u>multicultural</u>.

1. An area of a city is called a n_____.
2. People who travel around and teach about their god are m_____.
3. A place where people pray to a god is a c_____.
4. Something that is related to traditions and beliefs from many different countries is m_____.
5. A group of people who live in the same area form a c_____.
6. People who move to another country to live are i_____.
7. People from Central or South America are also known as L_____.

a. sing in the choir   **c.** play music
b. paint murals   **d.** eat Latin-American food

San Francisco's Mission Dolores church was built in 1791.

Each Sunday, people can hear the music of the Mission Dolores church in San Francisco. With the sound comes memories of the Spanish missionaries who built the church in 1791. They didn't know it at the time, but it was the start of a special type of neighbourhood: the Mission District.

The area is a place with a long and varied history. One member of the community describes it as a central part of San Francisco, because it's near where the city began long ago. He adds that it's important for people to understand the many levels of history in the neighbourhood. He feels that this knowledge is a big part of understanding what it means to be a real San Franciscan.

Fact Check: True or false?

1. The Mission District started in 1791.

2. Spanish missionaries built the church.

3. The Mission District has many layers of history.

One of the most interesting parts of the Mission District is its people. Over the years, immigrants have come to the area from Ireland, Germany, and Italy. But the most recent immigrants are mainly from Mexico and other countries in Central and South America. It's easy to see the style that these recent additions give the neighbourhood. You can see it in the art on the walls, taste it in the food, and hear it in the music.

Juan Pedro Gaffney grew up in the Mission District. He's the director of the Spanish Choir of San Francisco. In the past, his group has performed to raise money for people after **natural disasters**[1] in Central America. Many people in the choir are very close to these countries. Juan Pedro explains that the people in the Mission District share the pain and the happiness of their friends and relatives in Latin America. He says that the local **community**[2] feels a sense of common **involvement**[3]. They really care when a neighbouring nation is in pain.

---

[1] **natural disaster:** natural event that causes a lot of damage and serious problems
[2] **community:** all the people living in a particular area
[3] **involvement:** the act of taking part in an activity or a situation

During happy and sad times, the music produced in The Mission deeply affects everyone. Sometimes it helps people to share their sadness. Sometimes it helps them to enjoy life. Juan Pedro explains that music has always been an important part of the **cultural identity**[1] in The Mission. He feels that the music of the district is colourful and lively. According to him, it's absolutely '**jumping**[2]'.

It isn't just the music that's colourful and lively in the Mission District. The art of The Mission is full of life as well.

---

[1] **cultural identity:** sense of closeness to one's culture and environment
[2] **jumping:** *(slang)* very fun and lively

Canción, como un Disparo, Como un Libro
una ... rilla, Como Dyy el Amor,
... te Like a Book,
Love.

The local art community of The Mission stays close to the area's culture and tradition. A local arts organisation often leads people on walks through the district. They visit streets like Balmy Alley, which is famous for its **murals**[1].

Artist Ray Patlan talks about the art of the Mission District. 'What happens is, the murals begin to reflect the community itself,' he says. In 1984, Patlan helped to organise a group of artists to paint a series of murals here. The **theme**[2] at the time was 'Peace in Central America'.

---

[1] **mural:** a large wall painting
[2] **theme:** a central idea in a piece of art

Nowadays however, while the district remains mainly Latino, it is no longer 1984. The political situation is no longer the same. Patlan points out that both politics and the world have changed over the years. He then adds that because of this, the art in The Mission has changed as well. He explains that the art of the area is part of the streets, and it's also a **reflection**[1] of the community. So, as the community changes, people can see changes in the murals as well.

Even though the meanings behind the murals are always changing, they are still very powerful. **Apparently**[2], they're something the community likes a lot. Andrea Coombes lives in The Mission. 'It's great,' she says. 'It's like coming home to a piece of art every day. Every time we drive up it's just very **vibrant**!'[3]

---

[1]**reflection:** sth showing what another thing is like
[2]**apparently:** when sth seems to be true
[3]**vibrant:** lively and interesting

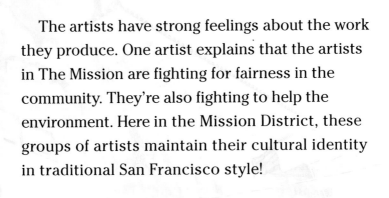

The artists have strong feelings about the work they produce. One artist explains that the artists in The Mission are fighting for fairness in the community. They're also fighting to help the environment. Here in the Mission District, these groups of artists maintain their cultural identity in traditional San Francisco style!

Many of these artists feel that The Mission is a successful neighbourhood where new immigrants are welcome. 'People see that they're not so different from each other,' says one artist. 'There [are] a lot of things that **bind**[1] [the immigrants] through culture and tradition.'

---

[1] **bind:** unite; bring together

The members of Saint Peter's Church are another group that understands the closeness between culture and tradition. Mission Dolores was the **foundation**[1] of the Mission District, but Saint Peter's is another strong base in the area.

Father Dan McGuire is the leader of Saint Peter's. He talks about all the different cultures that form the community around the church. 'The beauty of this particular **parish**[2],' says Father McGuire, 'is that the different cultures from Latin America and the different countries of Latin America come together here. And they really form a common unity.' The people who go to the church are from countries such as Mexico, El Salvador, and Peru. They come from all over Latin America!

---

[1]**foundation:** starting point; base
[2]**parish:** an area that has its own church

SAN
FRANCISCO
(MISSION
DOLORES)   CALIFORNIA

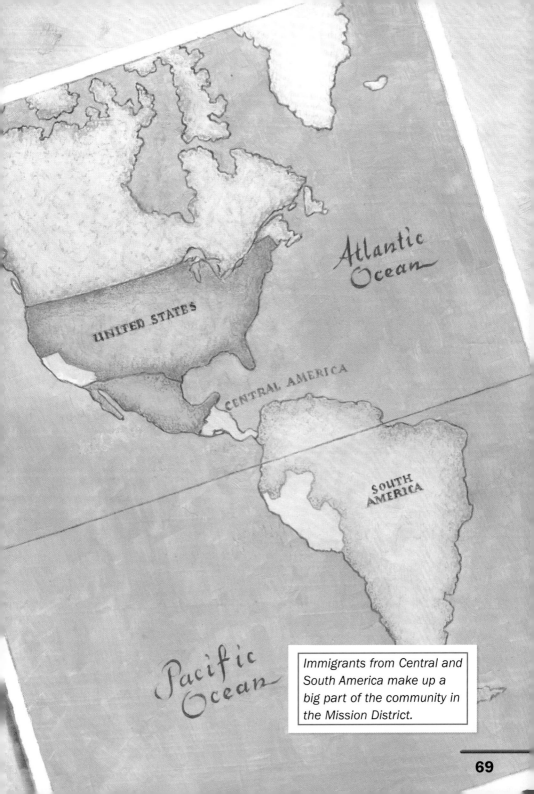

Atlantic Ocean

UNITED STATES

CENTRAL AMERICA

SOUTH AMERICA

Pacific Ocean

Immigrants from Central and South America make up a big part of the community in the Mission District.

Father McGuire talks about the success of new **immigrants**[1] in the area. 'They bring with them the best of their own country: particularly their interest in their families [and] their interests in their traditions,' he says. 'And what I see going on here in a very, very positive way is an **integration**[2] of the best of Latin American culture, now with American culture,' he adds.

In the Mission District, people are often able to fit into a new society very easily. Why? Because the environment of The Mission is so comfortable for them. It may be this comfortable feeling that helps to make this multicultural area such a very special kind of neighbourhood!

---

[1] **immigrant:** sb who has come to live in a country from another country
[2] **integration:** combination of; mixing with

How About You?

1. Would you like to live in, or visit, the Mission District? Why or why not?

2. What is your favourite thing about The Mission?

After You Read

1. The Mission District is a lively area of San Francisco.
   A. True
   B. False

2. On page 57, 'they' in the first paragraph refers to:
   A. people at church on Sunday
   B. missionaries in 1791
   C. people in Mission Delores
   D. people living in San Francisco

3. Which is a good heading for page 59?
   A. Strong Cultural Identity in Neighbourhood
   B. Juan Pedro Gaffney's German Choir
   C. Always Raising Money
   D. Juan Pedro Gaffney Moves to Area

4. On page 60, the word 'deeply' can be replaced by:
   A. really
   B. badly
   C. only
   D. lively

5. When does the music of the Mission District affect people?
   A. When they are happy.
   B. When they are enjoying life.
   C. When they are sad.
   D. all of the above

6. According to page 64, what does Ray Patlan think is important about the murals?
   A. They are very colourful.
   B. They were all painted in 1984.
   C. They are only about peace.
   D. They reflect the people and times.

7. On page 64, 'it's' in the first paragraph refers to:
    A. politics
    B. art
    C. community
    D. music

8. A good heading for page 67 is:
    A. Mission Artists Fight for Fairness
    B. Mission Artists Only Fight for Environment
    C. Style Missing in Mission District
    D. New Immigrants Sometimes Welcome

9. The Mission is a lively and interesting neighbourhood
    _____ many different people.
    A. where
    B. from
    C. in
    D. with

10. On page 68, the word 'foundation' in the first paragraph can be replaced by:
    A. culture
    B. house
    C. base
    D. parish

11. Father Dan McGuire believes that people in the Mission District:
    A. have formed a community around the church.
    B. are only from Mexico.
    C. should always come to his parish.
    D. come from Saint Peter's.

12. Which word best describes the Mission District?
    A. colourful
    B. loud
    C. Latino
    D. multicultural

A New Berlin

The old Berlin was known for its fine music, food, and art. Its streets were full of historical buildings and there were beautiful views everywhere. However, for 28 years, from 1961 to 1989, the city was divided into East and West Berlin by the Berlin Wall. This wall separated two areas that were controlled by different powers. During this time, Berlin lost some of its liveliness.

Nowadays, the city has many immigrant groups and a rising art and music culture. Berlin has become one of the most vibrant, multicultural cities in Europe. Today, about 3.5 million people live there. Half a million of these people were not born in Germany. These immigrants have come from 185 different countries. Many live in communities with other people from their homelands. Each of these neighbourhoods is a great place to see and each has a very different look and feel.

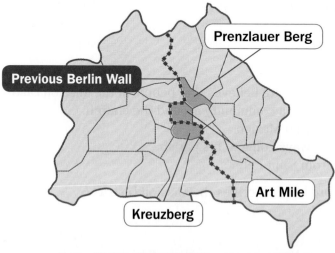

Some Multicultural Neighbourhoods of Berlin

Each year, thousands of people attend Berlin's art fairs.

Kreuzberg

Many people from the country of Turkey now live in the area of Kreuzberg. This is a lively area. In addition to all the special foods from Turkey and the bookstores, you will also find nightclubs here. In these clubs, people from many different cultures come together to play music and dance at night.

Art Mile

In the recent past, most artists lived and worked in West Berlin. But today everything has changed. The 'Art Mile' was an area in East Berlin that wasn't very interesting in the past. It is now the city's lively art centre. Berlin has two international art events in the 'Art Mile.' These events attract thousands of visitors from around the world each year.

Prenzlauer Berg

Visitors love the neighbourhood called Prenzlauerberg. Its streets are jumping with the energy of all the musicians, artists, and designers who live and work there. But there are also quiet, restful shops where people drink tea, read books, or write their own stories.

Word Count: 324
Time: _____

Grammar Focus: Present Perfect Continuous and Present Perfect

■ You use the present perfect for the present result of past actions, or with stative verbs. It expresses the connection between past events or situations, and the present or future.
I have worked at four different jobs in my life.

■ You use the present perfect continuous for actions that began in the past and continue now. It emphasises duration.
I have been working at this job for six years.

■ In some cases the two tenses can be used interchangeably.
I have been working on this report for a month, and I still haven't finished.
I have worked on this report for a month, and I still haven't finished.

Present Perfect: subject + have/has + past participle

I/You/They	have	read three books this month.
Bill/She	has	visited the museum many times.
		eaten Mongolian food.

Present Perfect Continuous: subject + have/has + been + present participle

I/You/They	have	been	playing tennis since three o'clock.
Bill/She	has		waiting for three hours.
			living here since 2002.
			working there for a long time.

Grammar Practice: Present Perfect Continuous and Present Perfect

Read the sentences and circle the answers to the questions.
1. 'Laura has been reading that book for three weeks.'
    Has Laura finished the book?   Yes   No
2. 'Jason played on the school basketball team.'
    Is Jason a member of the basketball team now?   Yes   No

Grammar Focus: Future: 'will'

■ Use *will* + base form of the verb to talk about what you think will happen in the future.

■ To form a contraction, use *'ll (I'll, you'll, he'll, she'll, we'll, they'll)*

People			
Students	will	fly to Mars.	
I	won't	study on the Internet	in the future.
He	(= will not)	find a cure for cancer	
We			

Grammar Practice: Future: 'will'

Write one thing you will do, and one thing you won't do, for each of these times.

1. tonight   _I will study for a test. I won't see my friends._

2. tomorrow   _____

3. next school vacation   _____

4. next year   _____

Grammar Focus: Direct Speech

- In writing, direct speech is used to indicate a speaker's exact words. It usually includes a reporting verb in either the simple present or simple past tense, along with quotation marks around the speaker's words.
- Commas are used to separate a speaker's words from the reporting phrase.
- A capital letter is used inside the quotation marks at the beginning of a speaker's sentence. For example:
  'People see that they're not so different from each other,' says one artist.
  Father McGuire said, 'They bring with them the best of their own countries.'

Grammar Practice: Direct Speech

Add quotation marks, commas, and capital letters where they are necessary.

1. People see that they're not so different from each other says one artist.
   'People see that they're not so different from each other,' says one artist.

2. It's a central part of the city says one member of the community

   _____

3. Father McGuire says they bring with them a strong interest in their families.

   _____

4. Juan Pedro explains the local community feels a sense of common involvement when a neighbour nation is in pain.

   _____

Video Practice

A. Watch the entire video of *Living with a Volcano* and make short notes so you can describe the volcano OR the towns near it.

_____

_____

_____

B. Watch Part 1 of the video again and circle the word you hear.
1. 'When Sicily's Mount Etna erupts, it really is a beautiful (sight/show).'
2. 'Mount Etna, or simply "Etna", is more than 10,000 feet high, which makes it (the world's/Europe's) highest active volcano.'
3. 'Caffo grew up in the city of Catania, less than 30 miles from Etna's (craters/top).'
4. 'On Etna, there are more than 100 craters and cones in a (huge/big) volcanic area.'
5. 'Today, thousands of people live on and (around/near) the volcano.'

C. Watch Part 2 of the video again and write down the word you hear.
1. 'There are over 20 small towns which lie around the _____ of the volcano.'
2. 'People go there to give thanks that the town was _____.'
3. 'In fact, according to Caffo, volcanoes are an important part of the world's _____ system.'
4. 'He explores the black land that is covered with hardened lava and _____ the ancient craters.'
5. 'The pressure was so powerful that lava shot a quarter of a mile into the _____!'

D. Watch the entire video of *Life on the Orinoco* and choose the main idea.
1. The Orinoco rain forest has some of the strangest animals in the world.
2. Many Indians of the Orinoco River still live in a traditional way.
3. The Orinoco is a special place, and people in Venezuela want to preserve it.

E. Watch Part 1 of the video again and circle the word you hear.
1. 'The Orinoco River is one of the longest rivers in (South America/the world.)'

2. 'On its way south, the Orinoco flows (through/around) many different landscapes.'
3. 'About two (hundred/thousand) Yanomami people live near the river, far from the modern world.'
4. 'The rainforest around the Orinoco River also has many plants and (animals/trees).'

F. Watch Part 2 of the video again and fill in the word or words.
1. 'However, over the past fifty years things have _____ along the Orinoco.'
2. 'Parts of the Orinoco now have dams to help control the _____.'
3. 'Now, very big ships now _____ up and down the river from the Atlantic Ocean to move these products.'

G. Watch the video of *A Special Type of Neighbourhood* and answer the questions.
1. What are the people inside the churches doing?

2. What does Juan Pedro Gaffney look like? What can you see him doing in the video?

H. Read the sentences. Then watch the video again and circle the word or words you hear.
1. 'Some community members describe the (neighbourhood/community) as a central part of the city.'
2. 'Over the years, (immigrants/travellers) have come here from Ireland, Germany, and Italy.'
3. 'In the past, the group has performed to (raise/make) money for people suffering after natural disasters in Central America.'

I. Watch the video again and answer the questions.
1. How is art a reflection of the community in the Mission District?

2. What countries do the people at Saint Peter's church come from?

3. Why can new immigrants to the Mission District live there easily?

(1) More than 10,000 feet in height, Mount Etna is Europe's tallest active volcano. (2) It began to form about 600,000 years ago at a place where two large tectonic plates meet. (3) Today you can see over 100 craters and cones in the area. (4) The rich volcanic dirt near Etna makes excellent farmland. (5) Also, tourists are attracted to the site. (6) For these reasons, many people choose to live in the area. (7) Some even live on the volcano itself. (8) The town of Nicolosi is 12 miles from the crater. (9) In the 800 years since it was built, Etna has destroyed it twice. (10) The people know that there is some risk involved in living so close to the volcano. (11) However, they say that if their town is destroyed, they will just rebuild it. (12) I wouldn't be comfortable living so close to an active volcano, but I'm glad that they are.

1. What do you think the best ending for this sentence would be? The people of Nicolosi

   _____.
   A. all work in the tourist industry
   B. aren't afraid of the volcano
   C. plan to rebuild their town soon
   D. live in a large crater

2. Where should this sentence go? It is also one of the oldest.
   A. after sentence 1
   B. after sentence 4
   C. after sentence 6
   D. after sentence 10

3. Another term for the earth's surface is its _____.
   A. volcanic ash
   B. lava
   C. crust
   D. magma

4. The word some in sentence 7 refers to _____.

Read the sentences. Write 'True' or 'False'. Refer to the paragraph if necessary.

5. The many large, moving pieces under the earth's surface are called craters. _____
6. The volcanic ash in the earth near to Mount Etna makes the ground hard. _____

(1) Life along the Orinoco River is changing. (2) Some towns and cities have become much larger, starting about fifty years ago. (3) Many new industries have come to the area. (4) Some of them produce gold, diamonds, and oil. (5) Today large ships travel up and down the Orinoco River. (6) In some places people have built dams to control the water. (7) These new dams also help to produce electricity. (8) There have been a lot of changes. (9) However, some areas are protected so no industry can develop there. (10) These areas are called national parks. (11) The parks help support the birds, animals, and people that live near the river.

7. According to the paragraph, when did development begin in the area?
   A. a hundred years ago
   B. fifty years ago
   C. ten years ago
   D. five years ago

8. Where should this sentence go? They carry these products to other countries.
   A. after sentence 2
   B. after sentence 4
   C. after sentence 5
   D. after sentence 9

9. Which animal is like a large cat?
   A. the jaguar
   B. the anaconda
   C. the crocodile
   D. piranha

10. _____ is a large area of flat land.
    A. A waterfall
    B. A mountain
    C. A plain
    D. A stream

11. Which sentence is correct?
    A. Who will to visit the park?
    B. Who will going to visit the park?
    C. Who will visiting the park?
    D. Who will visit the park?

(1) There are many attractive things about the Mission District in San Francisco. **(2)** First of all, there is lively music everywhere. **(3)** The Spanish Choir of San Francisco, led by Juan Pedro Gaffney, presents public performances. **(4)** They sometimes use these performances to raise money for people suffering natural disasters in Central America. **(5)** The district is full of beautiful art too. **(6)** The wall paintings in Balmy Alley are the work of some of the artists who live in the neighbourhood. **(7)** These murals are very special to the people of the Mission. **(8)** As artist Ray Paltan says, 'The murals begin to reflect the community itself.' **(9)** Although the Mission Dolores Basilica is older, Saint Peter's Church is also a very important place. **(10)** Father Dan McGuire is the leader of St. Peter's Church. **(11)** He says the new immigrants in the area are successful because they bring with them an interest in family and tradition. **(12)** In addition, the comfortable environment of this multicultural neighbourhood helps people feel at home.

12. The main idea of the reading is that _____.
   A. many new immigrants live in the Mission District
   B. a lot of artists live in the Mission District
   C. there are many reasons people like living in the Mission District
   D. there are two important churches in the Mission District

13. Where should this sentence go? People from that area care about others who still live there.
   A. after sentence 2
   B. after sentence 4
   C. after sentence 7
   D. after sentence 9

14. Immigrants are _____.
   A. Latino people
   B. people who come from Central and South America
   C. people who move to another country to live
   D. religious people

15. Some people in the Mission District _____ murals.
   A. play
   B. sing
   C. paint
   D. sell

16. Choose the correct sentence.
   A. Mark said, 'I want to see the murals.'
   B. 'I want to see the murals.' said Mark.
   C. Mark said 'I want to see the murals.'
   D. 'I want to see the murals' said Mark.

Key 答案

Living with a Volcano

Words to Know: A. 1. lava 2. crater 3. eruption 4. cones 5. magma
B. 1. volcanologists 2. tectonic plates 3. crust 4. volcanic ash 5. unpredictable
Skim for Gist: (suggested answers) 1. Mount Etna, a volcano in Italy 2. He is a scientist who studies Mount Etna. **Infer Meaning:** (suggested answers) 1. the people who live around Mount Etna 2. people and nature live closely together.
Sequence the Event: 2, 4, 1, 3 **After You Read: 1.** D **2.** A **3.** B **4.** C **5.** A **6.** C **7.** A **8.** B **9.** D **10.** C **11.** A **12.** B

Life on the Orinoco

Words to Know: A. (from left to right) 5. waterfall 3. mountain 8. rain forest 6. river 7. stream 1. sea 4. plain 2. delta **B. 1.** jaguar **2.** capybara **3.** crocodile **4.** anaconda **5.** piranha **Scan for Information: 1.** river **2.** river **3.** rainforest **4.** plains **Identify the Main Idea:** (suggested answers) 1. Over the past 50 years, things have changed along the Orinoco River. 2. Some cities and towns have grown a lot; these cities have taken land from animals and plants.
After You Read: 1. C **2.** D **3.** B **4.** D **5.** C **6.** B **7.** A **8.** A **9.** A **10.** C **11.** D

A Special Type of Neighbourhood

Words to Know: 1. neighbourhood **2.** missionaries **3.** church **4.** multicultural **5.** community **6.** immigrants **7.** Latino **B.** (From left to right) **a** (sing in choir), **c** (play music), **d** (eat Latin-American food), **b** (paint murals)
Fact Check: 1. True **2.** True **3.** True **How About You?:** Open answers
After You Read: 1. A **2.** B **3.** A **4.** A **5.** D **6.** D **7.** B **8.** A **9.** D **10.** C **11.** A **12.** D

Grammar Practice

Present Perfect Continuous and Present Perfect: 1. no **2.** no
Direct Speech: 2. 'It's a central part of the city,' says one member of the community. **3.** Father McGuire says, 'They bring with them a strong interest in their families.' **4.** Juan Pedro explains, 'The local community feels a sense of common involvement when a neighbour nation is in pain.'

Video Practice

B. 1. sight **2.** Europe's **3.** craters **4.** huge **5.** around **C. 1.** bottom **2.** saved **3.** environmental **4.** examines **5.** air **D.** 3 **E. 1.** the world **2.** through **3.** thousand **4.** animals **F. 1.** changed **2.** water **3.** travel **G.** (suggested answers) 1. People inside are singing, and one baby is playing. 2. He looks middle-aged. He has a moustache and wears glasses. He is singing, talking, and riding a bicycle. **H. 1.** neighbourhood **2.** immigrants **3.** raise **I.** (suggested answers) 1. As the community changes the art changes, too. 2. They come from countries such as Mexico, El Salvador, and Peru. 3. New immigrants can live there easily because of the comfortable environment of the Mission District.

Exit Test

1. B **2.** A **3.** C **4.** people **5.** F **6.** F **7.** B **8.** C **9.** A **10.** C **11.** D **12.** C **13.** B **14.** C **15.** C **16.** A

English - Chinese Vocabulary List 中英對照生詞表

(Arranged in alphabetical order)

anaconda	大蟒蛇	**mayor**	市長 / 鎮長
ancient	古老	**mural**	壁畫
apparently	顯然的	**natural disaster**	自然災害
bind	使連接	**natural resource**	天然資源
community	社區	**paddle**	划槳
(be) conscious of	意識到	**parish**	教區
cultural identity	文化認同	**piranha**	食人鯧
dam	堤壩	**reflection**	反映
erupt	爆發	**religious statue**	宗教雕像
foundation	基礎	**reserve**	保護區
immigrant	（外來）移民	**rodent**	嚙齒類（如老鼠）
integration	整合	**scare**	使恐懼
interaction	互相影響	**shivers down (one's) spine**	顫抖
involvement	參與	**sulphur**	硫磺
jaguar	美洲豹	**theme**	主題
jumping	生動有趣	**thermodynamic**	熱力學（的）
landscape	景色	**tributary**	支流
leave (sth) out of the equation	置之不理	**vibrant**	充滿生氣的